BOWLING

Written By:
Herbert I. Kavet

Illustrated By:
Martin Riskin

© 1992
by **Ivory Tower Publishing Company, Inc.**
All Rights Reserved

No portion of this book may be reproduced - mechanically, electronically, or by any other means including photocopying - without the permission of the publisher.

Manufactured in the United States of America

30 29 28 27 26 25 24 23 22 21 20 19 18 17 16 15 14 13 12 11 10 9 8 7 6 5 4 3 2 1

Ivory Tower Publishing Co., Inc.
125 Walnut Street
P.O. Box 9132
Watertown, MA 02272-9132
Telephone #: (617) 923-1111   Fax #: (617) 923-8839

"Johnny was stretching to warm up and threw out his back."

"If I wanted advice on my form, I would have brought my wife to videotape me."

"Mind if I finish my frames all at once? I'm getting married at noon."

"It seems reasonable to assume an expensive ball should be more accurate than a cheap one."

"I think Sid's fallen asleep."

"We all just bowl to relax."

"I like Jimmy. He always knows when he's had enough to drink."

"No one is laughing at you."

"The big bag theory of incompetence."

"It's no use sulking, Harry. Everyone has an off day."

"Honey, have you seen my bowling shoes?"

"I can't stand women who show off."

"Me? I'm in life insurance."

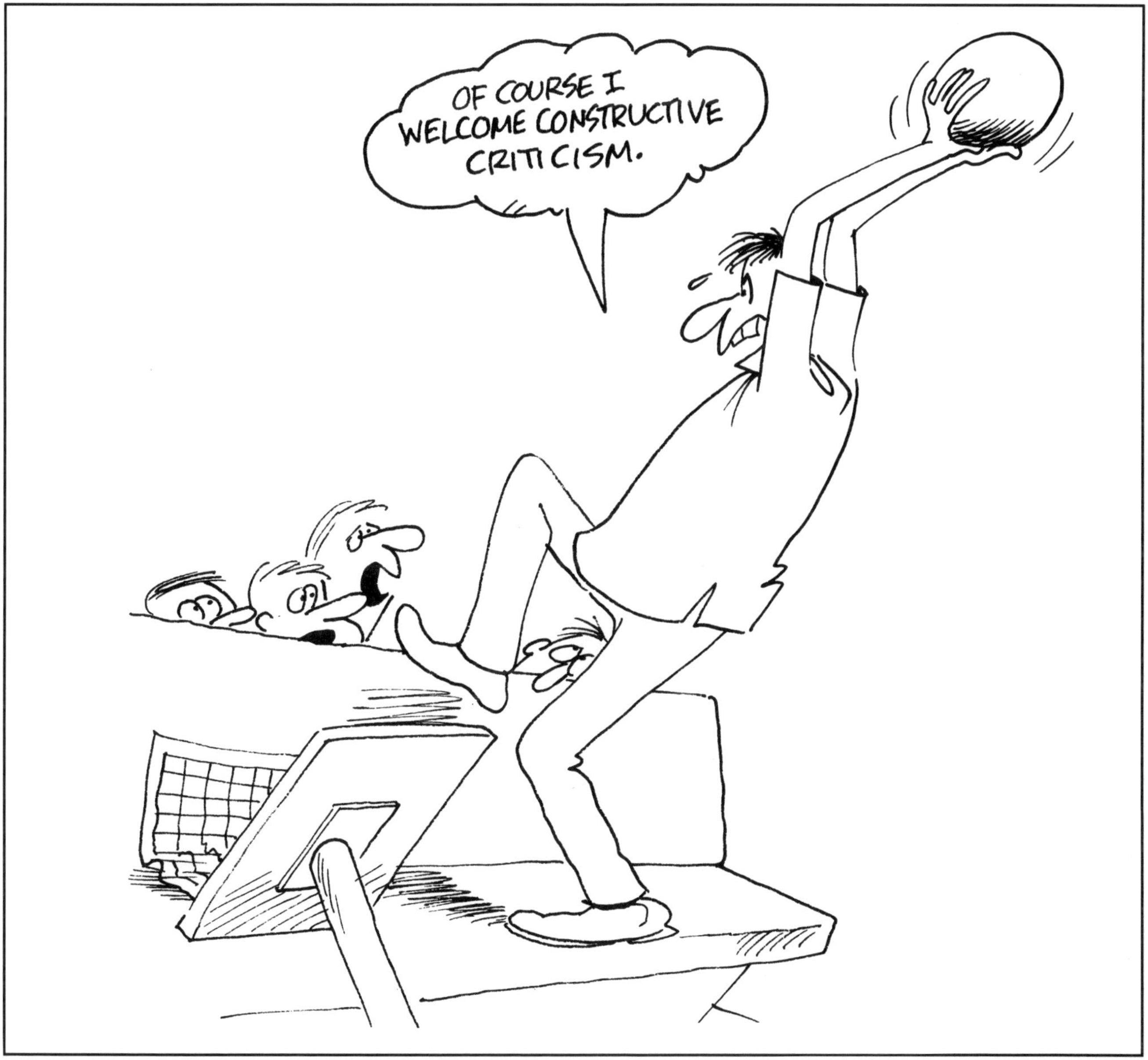
OF COURSE I WELCOME CONSTRUCTIVE CRITICISM.

"Sid, stop distracting my partners."

"Honey, I finally bowled a 300."

"Dear, I think your hair is thinning on top."

"For God's sake, Kevin, I'll buy you a beer. Stop embarrassing everyone on the team."

"Impossible as it sounds, there are evidently some people who can send the ball all the way down the alley and not hit a single pin."

"Andy is such a sore loser."

"Remember, Al, stay loose in the approach."

"Tony really has one hell of a hook."

"The ghost of open frames past."

"Willie's playing so bad tonight he's thinking of giving up beer."

"Gloria wasn't quite satisfied with the approach."

"What's going on up there?"

"Joey, where's your sportsmanship?"

"Where in blazes is my bowling ball?"

"Herman has perfected the 7 step delivery."

"Eyes on the head pin."

"Father, that's not fair."

"Oh, another one for the hall of fame."

"Happy birthday, darling."

"I trust you have that lofting problem a bit under control, Mr. Benson."

"Now, watch Howie 'steer' the ball right into the pocket."

"Sorry about that."

"Josh, you're holding up the game."

Fat Finger Freddie learns the proper way to pick up a ball.

"I understand she's an outrageous tipper."

"Have some more relaxer, Murray."

"Debbie, will you keep Scott under control!"

"It's all right, it's all right. I'm just showing him."

"It ain't orthodox, but he's our leading scorer."

"I still say it's not fair."

"Big battle, many cannon."

"Fred's having a hot night and carrying the team."

Evolution of bowling by trial and error.

When bowlers get disgusted with their game.

"Brian's going to wet his pants."

"Cut that out, Merlin, or no one's going to want to play with you."

Al has a real presence on the lanes.

Where score sheet cheaters end up.

"You did not let me win just because it's my birthday."

"Phil is accurate enough. He just has to put a little more speed on the ball."

"We were totally happy for six years — out of 23 that was."

"Try for a little more distance, Shirley."

"Concentrating? Hell, I think he's got gas."

"I see the Rockets have completed their
pre-game warm-up."

"Has anyone seen Warren?"

"Relax, Charlie, one more ball and you'll have bowled a perfect game."

"Vern's coaching really goes too far."

Sal finds the hardest part of bowling is turning to face his team.

These other books are available at many fine stores.

#2350 Sailing. Using the head at night • Sex & Sailing • Monsters in the Ice Chest • How to look nautical in bars and much more nautical nonsense.

#2351 Computers. Where computers really are made • How to understand computer manuals without reading them • Sell your old $2,000,000 computer for $60 • Why computers are always lonely and much more solid state computer humor.

#2352 Cats. Living with cat hair • The advantages of kitty litter • Cats that fart • How to tell if you've got a fat cat.

#2353 Tennis. Where do lost balls go? • Winning the psychological game • Catching your breath • Perfecting wood shots.

#2354 Bowling. A book of bowling cartoons that covers: Score sheet cheaters • Boozers • Women who show off • Facing your team after a bad box and much more.

#2355 Parenting. Understanding the Tooth Fairy • 1000 ways to toilet train • Informers and tattle tales • Differences between little girls and little boys • And enough other information and laughs to make every parent wet their beds.

#2356 Fitness. T-shirts that will stop them from laughing at you • Earn big money with muscles • Sex and Fitness • Lose weight with laughter from this book.

#2357 Golf. Playing the psychological game • Going to the toilet in the rough • How to tell a real golfer • Some of the best golf cartoons ever printed.

#2358 Fishing. Handling 9" mosquitoes • Raising worms in your microwave oven • Neighborhood targets for fly casting practice • How to get on a first name basis with the Coast Guard plus even more.

#2359 Bathrooms. Why people love their bathroom • Great games to help pass the time on toilets • A frank discussion of bathroom odors • Plus lots of other stuff everyone out of diapers should know.

#2360 Biking. Why the wind is always against you • Why bike clothes are so tight • And lots of other stuff about what goes thunk, thunk, thunk when you pedal.

#2361 Running. How to "go" in the woods • Why running shoes cost more than sneakers • Keeping your lungs from bursting by letting the other guy talk.

Ivory Tower Publishing Co., Inc.   125 Walnut St., PO Box 9132, Watertown, MA 02272-9132
Telephone #: (617) 923-1111   Fax #: (617) 923-8839